Understanding the Five-Fold Ministry: Five-Fold Ascension Gifts

THERESA A. BUCKNER

DEDICATION

This book is dedicated to all that are assigned and appointed to the five-fold ministry by God. To every Kingdom Citizen serving in advancing the Kingdom of God. .

CONTENTS

Acknowledgments i

1 Equipping 1

2 The Apostle 11

3 The Prophet 25

4 The Evangelist 38

5 The Pastor 45

6 The Teacher 54

ACKNOWLEDGMENTS

I would like to acknowledge my Lord and Savior Jesus Christ, my husband Bishop Herbert Buckner, my pastor Apostle John Eckhardt, and the many men and women of God that have poured into my life. I am grateful for the sacrifice that my husband and children make as I continue to pour my life out in service to the LORD. I would like to acknowledge every member of Divinely Inspired Ministry International Fellowship, and all those that continue to pray for me. God bless you all.

1 EQUIPPING

Ephesians 4:11-13 (NKJV)

And He Himself gave some to be apostles, some prophets, some evangelists, and some pastors and teachers, for the equipping of the saints for the work of ministry, for the edifying of the body of Christ, till we all come to the unity of the faith and of the knowledge of the Son of God, to a perfect man, to the measure of the stature of the fullness of Christ;

Throughout the history of the church, we have seen many

different governing offices erected in place to lead the people. We have seen leadership models similar to dictatorship, corruption, power abusers, and those that have truly care for the people of God. There are also those who advocate a lack of governmental order and structure within the church, and those that operate within a governing system where everyone participates. We see elections, councils, and similar structures of authority over the years, active and ready modern leadership. What we often don't see is the structure of governing put into place in the New Testament. The New Testament structure of ministry leadership is the structure that Christ left for His church. It balances authority for full covering of the church, rather than enabling power to be within the hands of one or only a few leaders. The Kingdom of God offers a new approach to leadership, and qualifications to be in leadership.

Understanding the function and purpose of the Five-Fold Ministry within the Church is important, because it enables us to work efficiently and effectively together as a collective body of believers working together in unity. We must work together in unity as we continue to strive to become a mature body in Christ. Throughout the Bible, the emphasis of unity and oneness is prevalent. There is a universal principle that exists about the power of agreement. In order for us to walk in agreement, we must walk in unity. Much is accomplished this way. The five-fold ministry governing structure set in the church by Christ was given to us as a pattern for structure, order, and function.

All five offices in operation within a local assembly is still yet to many a source of contention. Some claim that certain offices no longer exists, while others choose to stifle the operation of others. Many that say that certain five-fold offices such as the apostle and prophet are no longer evident use the following passage: **Hebrews 1:1-2** *God, who at sundry times and in divers manners spake in time past unto the fathers by the prophets, Hath in these last days spoken unto us by his Son, whom he hath appointed heir of all* *things, by whom also he made the worlds;* (New King James Version). Father God indeed did and continues to speak through Jesus Christ to His Bride. With further insight, this passage demonstrates the headship of Christ in the governance of the Church Age. If this passage means that Father God speaks to us through Jesus only now, we would have to eliminate all of the other office…and personal ministry to one another would be illegal operation.

Further evidence that the offices of the five-fold ministry are not eliminated within the church can be found within the passage of

Ephesians 4:7-13 *But unto every one of us is given grace according to the measure of the gift of Christ. Wherefore he saith, When he ascended up on high, he led captivity captive, and gave gifts unto men. (Now that he ascended, what is it but that he also descended first into the lower parts of the earth? He that descended is the same also that* *ascended up far above all heavens, that he might fill all things.) And*

he gave some, apostles; and some, prophets; and some, evangelists; and

some, pastors and teachers; For the perfecting of the saints, for the

work of the ministry, for the edifying of the body of Christ: Till we all

come in the unity of the faith, and of the knowledge of the Son of God,

unto a perfect man, unto the measure of the stature of the fullness of

Christ.

The passage above references that Jesus gave the five-fold ministry gifts measures of grace to operate, and lists each particular gift given for the governance of His church. The passage reveals that the gifts were given for the perfecting of the saints for the work of the ministry. Each gift is given a measure of grace to perfect the saints for the work of the ministry. The passage continues with stating that it is for the edifying of the body of Christ. The five-fold ministry gifts are given a measure of grace that edifies the body of Christ. This is till we all come in the unity of the faith, knowledge of the Son of God, unto a perfect man....unto a perfect man, unto the measure of the stature of the fullness of Christ. This claim does not apply, because this would mean that the body has reached full maturity, perfection, and edification with the work of the ministry being completed. The maturity of the church, perfection, edification, and the work of the ministry will not be completed until the 2nd coming of Christ.

The church as a whole body has not arrived at the place of maturity into one a perfect man operating within stature of the fullness of Christ. The offices of the apostles, prophets, evangelists, pastors, and teachers are gifts. They are a gift to the people assigned to the offices and to the church. People reject these offices by. Rejection of any of these offices in essence is rejection of gifts from God to His body. We (the church) have not reached and fulfilled the purposes of the five-fold ministry, and therefore cannot argue the validity of the five-fold ministry as being invalid. Rejection of one office would cause for elimination of all offices, because they were all given together.

The church as a whole is operating in an immature state. Part of the reason for the immaturity in the church is leadership which does not follow the leadership structure given by Jesus Christ Himself within the New Testament leadership. Attempting to eliminate Scriptural leadership offices, or trying to replace Scriptural offices with others causes dysfunction within the church. This leaves the church open to the invasion of false teachers as proper discernment for leadership becomes muddled. Some non-Biblical roles present in today's religions are papal offices, cardinals, and the Roman Curia. It is not appropriate to elect church leaders. It is not appropriate, because it does not follow the New Testament structure. When we try to eliminate or try to replace Scriptural offices with non-Scriptural ones, it leaves the church open to invasion false teachers, because proper discernment for leadership becomes muddled. 7. The offices of the five-fold ministry are to be executed in love. The purpose in the five-fold ministry is "to

bring together the body of Christ and give it to full maturity.

The offices edify the church by teaching the truth in love.

2 APOSTLES

"Whereto I am ordained a preacher, and an apostle (I speak the truth in Christ, and lie not); a teacher of the Gentiles in faith and verity. " (**1 Timothy 2:7**)

One of the most controversial offices within the time of its inception is that of the Apostle. The debate pertaining to apostles in modern times is not anything new and has been continued on since the inception of the original twelve. Many theological debates are not new, but have been going on since the beginning of the church. Apostles are definitely needed within the church today, just as they were needed within the church at the church's conception. The church is still in an immature state and not walking within the unity of the faith of Christ, which is evident by the various theological debates that have existed for a long time. We know in part and prophesy in part, therefore the time when all things will be made known will come only after the 2nd coming of Christ. Many refute and claim that this office has been eliminated, because the canonized Bible is complete. Some believe that this office is died out when the original 12 disciples/ambassadors of the Lamb died out. The office of the Apostle has been replaced many times by the office of Bishops and Pastors. Church history records how Bishops were appointed to oversee churches and ministries, and many took this as the eradication of the office of the Apostle. There is no Scriptural evidence to support the eradication of this office.

You cannot build the church upon a pastor; the apostle comes with the revelation of God for the right foundation and doctrine of the church (**Ephesians 2:20, Ephesians 4:11**).

Advocates of the pastoral church find the five-fold ministry threatening, due to issues of submitting to a leader and struggling with control issues. They may operate off of a power trip, dictator, or tyranny type of leadership style. Patriarchy is another threat to the Gospel and the Gospel understanding worldwide in that it is not based upon the New Testament structure of the church governance, which gives off a false representation of Christ's church. It also allows room for the invasion of false teachers to enter in and teach heretical doctrine and theology. Another issue with the patriarchal setup is that these types of churches rarely reach outside of themselves, which limits the spread of the Gospel to other nations. Without the office of the apostle, people will continue to misuse the Bible and misinterpret it, because it is the apostle that has the mysteries of God designed to teach the Body of Christ.

The term Apostle comes from the Greek word "apostolos",which means a delegate, messenger, one sent forth with orders. The word "apostle" means a delegate, an ambassador, a messenger with a special message, or one who is sent forth with orders. The office is received by grace with the power to represent Christ, as Christ was the first apostle sent to represent the Father (**John 12:46-50, Hebrews 3:1**). The apostle serves as God's ambassador, specifically commanded by God to go forth with the message of the Gospel (**Galatians 1:1**). The apostle is guardian of this message; sent to likewise ensure those who proclaim the Gospel in any office do not stray from the Gospel message. Apostles are both a minister and a witness to the grace received in Christ and the direct calling experienced and the faith learned by revelation of Christ (**Acts 26:14-18**).

Two sets of criteria supported biblically exists for those functioning within the office of the apostle. The of these required of apostles is that they must have followed Christ throughout His earthly ministry, and after the resurrection.

These types of apostles are referred to as apostles of the Lamb. This particular criteria served to elect a replacement for Judas after his suicide. The selection of Matthias was done under this criteria, through which the apostles cast lots (**Acts 1:13-26**).

The second set of criteria biblically supported for those functioning within the office of the apostle can be seen through the apostleship of Saul turned Paul (**Acts 9**). This is the standard for the apostolic office unto this day, as it is the calling for apostles of the New Covenant. One must be called of God to be an apostle directly through Jesus Christ. They must have an experience with the resurrected Christ. They are to be taught by Christ through the revelation. They are to be sent by Christ for the work of the Gospel. Apostles must have a thorough knowledge of the Scriptures. The ministry of the apostle is proven by their teaching, preaching, and ministry work of the Gospel. The standard for today is the second set of criteria established with the call of the apostle Paul. The criteria as aforementioned to be an apostle are: called of God to be an apostle directly through Jesus Christ, have an experience with the resurrected Christ, be taught by Christ through revelation, be sent by Christ for the work of the Gospel, and have a thorough knowledge of Scripture.

> ➤ One must be called of God to be an apostle directly through Jesus Christ (**1 Corinthians 1:9, Galatians 1:1**).

> ➤ One must have an experience with the resurrected Christ (**Acts 26:14-18**).

> ➤ One must be taught by Christ through the revelation (**Romans 1:5, Galatians 1:11**).

> ➤ One must be sent by Christ for the work of the Gospel (**Ephesians 3:1-7**).

> ➤ One must have a thorough knowledge of Scriptures (**2 Timothy 2:15**).

The two sets of criteria that I have just mentioned are biblically supported. There are many other views in regards to the apostleship. However, I will only present biblically based evidence throughout this book. Yes, there are other convincing arguments out there about who and how in regards to the apostleship. I have only found these two criteria types that is supported substantially Scripturally. The establishment of an apostle comes from God alone and is proven through execution of that office.

As with any office or function, there are responsibilities that are set in place for the apostleship. This office and any other five-fold ministry office is received by grace with the power to represent Christ, as Christ was the first apostle to represent the Father. The Apostle as a guardian of the Gospel is sent to ensure that those who proclaim the message in any office do not stray from the Gospel message. The duties of the apostle are many and includes: guarding, teaching, and revealing the mysteries of Christ and remaining faithful with them, organizing, administrating, and working dutifully to establish the body; serve in the office of doctrinal establishment, correction and moral establishment and correction; train and educate church leaders; operating in the gifs of the Spirit; walk in prophetic offices and assess prophecy on a doctrinal level; work as a preacher and teacher for the church and to mixed or unbelieving groups as well, teach and baptize new members, pray for people to receive the gift of the Holy Ghost, and ordain others in the five-fold ministry to offices by the laying on of hands.

> ➤ Guarding, teaching, and revealing the mysteries of Christ (the revelation of Christ which is the foundation of the church) and remaining faithful with them (**1 Corinthians 4:1-2**)
> ➤ Organizing, administrating, and working dutifully to establish the body (**1 Corinthians 12:28**)

➤ Serve in the office of doctrinal establishment, correction, and moral establishment and correction (**Acts 2:42**)

➤ Train and educate church leaders; operating in the gifts of the Spirit (**Acts 5:12, 2 Corinthians 12:12**)

➤ Walk in the prophetic offices, and assess prophecy on a doctrinal level; work as a preacher and teacher for the church and to mixed or unbelieving groups as well (**1 Timothy 2:7, Acts 2:4-35, Acts 3:12-19**)

➤ Teach and baptize new members (**Acts 2:36-43**)

➤ Pray for people to receive the gift of the Holy Spirit (**Acts 8:14-17**)

➤ Ordain others in the five-fold ministry to offices by laying on of hands (**1 Timothy 5:22, 2 Timothy 1:6, Hebrews 6:2**)

Some of the people that served as apostles within the New Testament were the original twelve, Matthias, Paul, Mary

Magdalene, Timothy, Silvanus, Barnabas, Junia, and

Andronicus. Both men and women served as apostles. Biblical

examples of some that are clearly shown within Scriptures to be

Apostles are as follows (not all inclusive):

> The original 12 (**Matthew 10:1-3**)

> Matthias (**Acts 1:26**)

> Paul (**Acts 26:14-18**)

> Mary Magdalene (**Luke 24:10**)

> Timothy (**1 Thessalonians 1:1**)

> Silvanus (**1 Thessalonians 1:1**)

> Barnabas (**Acts 14:14**)

> Junia (**Romans 16:7**)

> Andronicus (**Romans 16:7**),

There are recorded within the Old and New Testament

Apostolic types of the apostle's ministry. Types serve as

examples of what an apostolic ministry looks like. It is very important that as we learn about the five-fold ministry that we understand what it looks like through the lens of Scripture. The following are biblical examples of types of apostolic ministry:

> **Genesis 12:1-6** Abram turned Abraham

> **Exodus 6:1-13:22** Moses

> **Joshua 1:1-18** Joshua

> **Judges 4:4-16** Deborah

> **Matthew 3:1-12, John 3:27-36** John the Baptist

The following is a list of characteristics that are perceivable about characteristics regarding some of the highly active biblical apostles:

> The Apostle Peter, **Acts 2:14-41**: Take charge, takes initiative, rise to the task to get things done, accept responsibility for their actions, teaching, and the call

of God on their lives, display clarity and truth in Gospel presentation; fully equipped to speak, write, and teach the Word; intense, can be harsh or punitive, yet stir conviction unto repentance.

➤ The Apostle Paul, **1 Corinthians 3-4**: Strong personalities, can clash in personality with others; may not always work well with others; apostles must remain humble, focused in God, and maintain truth in integrity; ability to solve problems (both their own and those pertaining to church ministry); constantly able to handle questions of doctrine, debate, and conflicts between individuals; able to teach in different situations; can deal with temper, frustration, and anger; push for and desire perfection; advocate standards difficult to meet.

➤ The Apostle James, **James 2:1-25**: Emphasize doing rather than just receiving; participate in life; respond head-on with enthusiasm and zeal; involved in faith.

➢ The Apostle John, **2 John 1-13**: Furiously independent in spirit; objective detachment needed to assess problems, difficulties, and doctrinal questions; loves deeply, displaying the love of Christ and the Father; do not desire to see others depart into error; stubborn, especially on essential church matters.

Within this chapter, you have been presented substantial biblical understanding for the office of the Apostle. It provides a foundational understanding of the office of the apostle to include the meaning, purpose, origins, duties, examples (biblical), and the criteria. Recognizing what the Bible reveals about this five-fold ministry gift by having Scriptural understanding will assist in bringing clarity to the hearts and minds of the people of God. It is wise to continue to seek the whole counsel of God through His Word, His Spirit, and other resources that may be available for further research and studies.

I encourage each one of you to be as the Bereans. Search the Scriptures to make sure that what is presented to you, so that you may prove according to the Word of God that it aligns with what God has revealed. You will be able to identify each by their fruit (the fruit of the Spirit), including the evidence of their ministry.

3 PROPHETS

Now therefore ye are no more strangers and foreigners, but fellow citizens

with the saints, and of the household of God; And are built upon the

foundation of the apostles and prophets, Jesus Christ himself being the chief

corner stone; In whom all the building fitly framed together groweth unto an

holy temple in the Lord: In whom ye also are builded together for an

habitation of God through the Spirit. (**Ephesians 2:19-22**)

Ephesians 2:19-22 expresses clearly the role of the apostles and

prophets in regards to church leadership. Within the church,

Jesus Christ is the chief corner stone, while the apostles and

prophets serve as the foundation of the church. The office of

the prophet continues to be a disputed functional office within church leadership. This is seen within many traditional evangelical circles that are structured with the leadership of the pastor as the foundation or set person. As written in **Ephesians 2 & 4**, the prophet plays a significant role within church leadership. As with the apostle, there isn't any scriptural evidence of the eradication of this particular office. Even though people argue that the prophetic era is over, this is unscriptural. If the testimony of Jesus is the spirit of prophecy, all prophecy should point to Christ (**Revelation 19:10**). Prophets remain a function within the church, and its leadership structure.

The office of the prophet is found both in the Old and New Testaments, and the requirements for the prophetic office remain the same. Prophets must be called of God, and not of human beings as the prophetic office is not one can receive by human appointment (**Isaiah 6:1-13**). A prophet must have a willing heart and tongue, must fully deliver the message God relays to them (**Acts 15:32-35**), have the discernment to recognize personal thoughts, perceptions, and opinions from the divine prophecy (**Jonah 1:1-3**), a heart of courage to speak God's will to whomever God sends them to (**Jeremiah 1: 1-10**), and the ability to discern between spirits (**1 John 4:1-3**). The office of prophet is a universal office. Prophets are not sent to serve in immediate locations alone, but are a gift to the universal body of believers. They may be sent with their message anywhere in the world (**Jeremiah 1:10**). The ministry of a prophet is proven by their words. If a prophet speaks what is true and their prophecies come true, then they are a true prophet. If they proclaim and prophesy falsehood, they are a false and should not be given heed (**Deuteronomy 18:15-22**). Prophesy is from the Greek word "propheteuo, which means, to prophesy, to be a prophet, speak forth by divine inspirations, to predict.

The office of the prophet also comes with another major controversy, due to the fact that all spirit filled and led believers possess the ability to prophesy. There is indeed a difference between the office of the prophet, and one who possess the ability to prophesy. The prophetic office is a part of the five-fold ministry. It must be appointed by God Himself. There is a difference between a prophetic gift and the prophetic office as found in the five-fold ministry. Anyone in the body of Christ can receive the gift of prophecy and can prophecy. It is a much sought after gift. The prophetic office is one by which one walks in a specific calling of God by grace for the foundation and building up of the church body. The word 'prophet' means one who speaks for God; a spokesman of God; an oracle of sacred or hidden things. The purpose of this office is to ensure that the church receives the message of God in this day and age and the revealing of the message for tomorrow. Prophets have many unique duties as pertain to their office, which help to guard the body of Christ spiritually with discernment.

Prophets must be called of God. The prophetic office is not one that can be received by human appointment. A prophet must have a willing heart and tongue, must fully deliver the message God relays to him or her, have the discernment to recognize personal thoughts, perceptions, and opinions from the divine prophecy, a heart of courage to speak God's will to whomever God sends them to speak, and the ability to discern between spirits.

- Must be called by God
- Must have a willing heart and tongue
- Must fully deliver God's message
- Must operate with discernment
- Must be courageous
- Must be able to discern spirits.

The office of the prophet comes with its own distinct duties in fulfilling its function as a foundation gift within the church. Prophets are to speak God's will to individuals, regions, nations, and the church (**Revelation 10:9-11**). They are to interpret current events in the light of Scriptural prophecy (**Daniel 7:1-15**). Prophets teach on prophetic matters, including the interpretation of Scriptural prophecy (**1 Peter 1:10-12**). Other duties are to discern spirits and prophetic words (**1 Corinthians 12:10, 1 John 4:1-3**). Furthermore prophets serves as seers and visionaries, and also interpret dreams, visions, signs and words of God to individuals (**Hosea 12:10**). Prophets are be heralds of God's judgment and grace (**Jeremiah 28:9, Jeremiah 44:4**). Other duties include: function in intercessory prayer and praise and worship (**2 Chronicles 32:20-23**); serve to deliver messages to God's people from God Himself (**2 Kings 22:14-20**); serve as a discerner of character, morals, and actions among believers (**Ezekiel 2:1-10**); walk in the gifts of the Spirit especially prophecy (**1 Corinthians 14:1**), and provide warning of times and divine correction from God and tell us what is to come (**Ezekiel 4:9-16**); be aware of natural phenomena in light of prophecy, and especially aware of God's judgment manifest through nature (**Joel 2:28-31**).

➢ Speaking God's will to individuals, regions, nations, and the entire body of believers

➢ Interpret current events in the light of Scriptural prophecy

➢ Teach on prophetic matters

➢ Discern spirits and prophetic words

➢ Serve as a seer and visionary

➢ Interpret dreams and visions

➢ Heralds of God's message of grace and judgment

➢ Intercessory Prayer

➢ Worship

➢ Provide warning

➢ Provide Divine correction

➢ Foretell

➢ Forth-tell

Many men and women throughout the Scriptures served in the office of prophet. They include:

➢ Miriam (**Exodus 15:20**)

➢ Deborah (**Judges 4:4-5**)

➢ Samuel (**1 Samuel 3:1-18**)

➢ Isaiah (**Isaiah 6:1-13**)

➢ Isaiah's wife (**Isaiah 8:3**)

➢ Ezekiel (**Ezekiel 2:1-10**)

➢ Jeremiah (**Jeremiah 1:1-10**)

➢ Daniel (**Daniel 2:25-26**)

➢ Hosea (**Hosea 1:1**)

➢ Moses (**Exodus 4:11**)

➢ Aaron (**Exodus 4:14-16**)

➢ Obadiah (**Obadiah 1:1**)

➢ Micah (**Micah 1:1**)

➢ Jonah (**Jonah 1:1-3**)

➢ Zechariah (**Zechariah 7:1-9**)

➢ Zephaniah (**Zephaniah 1:1**)

➢ Malachi (**Malachi 1:1**)

➢ Huldah (**2 Kings 22:14-20**)

➢ Anna (**Luke 2:36**)

➢ Four daughters of Philip (**Acts 21:9**)

There exists types of prophetic ministry levels. Spirit of prophecy is the most basic level (**Numbers 11:29; Acts 2:14-18, Revelation 19:10**) of prophetic ministry. At this level edification, exhortation, and comfort are expressed. The Word of God testifies of Jesus, and carries with it the spirit of prophecy.

The next type of prophetic ministry is that of the gift of

prophecy (**1 Corinthians 12:10**), which can be stirred up (**2 Timothy 1:6**). Those who prophesy out of this level will speak words that will bring edification, exhortation, and comfort (**1 Corinthians 14:3**). This is the highest level that someone that is not called into the office of the prophet should attempt to operate. We can operate in the gift of prophecy whenever we assemble as the people of God and, yet, still not be a prophet

The final level of prophetic ministry is the office of the prophet. The office of the prophet is the highest level in the prophetic realm (**1 Corinthians 12:28**). Prophets will have strong utterances, because they speak by the spirit of prophecy, the gift of prophecy, and also out of the strength of the prophet's office. Their messages go beyond words of edification, exhortation, and comfort. They prophesy with authority, rebuke, correction, revelation, direction, correction, confirmation, impartation, and activation.

There are various characteristics in regards to the office of the prophets. There are different administrations, but the same Lord (**1 Corinthians 12:5**), including the measure of grace given in regards to prophecy. All prophets do not flow within the same administration of the office. Some prophets are stronger in healing and miracles, others visions and dreams, others impartation, and others confirmation. Different administrations or applications to reach different people.

- ➢ Prophetic music (psalmists or minstrels) **1 Chronicles 25:1, 2 Samuel 23:1**
- ➢ Prophetic helps (builders) **Ezra 5:1-2, Haggai 1:2**
- ➢ Prophetic revelation **Amos 3:7**
- ➢ Shamar prophets serve through prophetic intercession, prophetic discernment, prophetic praise, prophetic preaching, prophetic teaching, and prophetic worship. Shamar means to guard, to keep,

to be a watchman. This prophet type is a guardian. The shamar prophet also builds a hedge of protection. Shamar means to guard, to keep, to be a watchman. They identify possible enemies. They seek God for strategies in how to resist, expel, and overcome these enemies in the power of the Holy Spirit.

➤ Nabi literally means "to bubble up." It describes one who is stirred up in spirit. It is the most frequently used of the three by the Hebrew writers. When the sense of "bubbling up" is applied to speaking, it becomes "to declare." Hence, a nabi, or a prophet, is an announcer—one who pours forth the declarations of God.

➤ Chozeh (Vision)-Going into a trance, open vision, counselor, advisor, wisdom

➤ Prophetes (To Foretell)-Future prediction

➤ Nataph (to preach)-tearing open heavens bringing

revelation. Freedom through energetic vocalized prophecies. Operate in fire. Burning

➤ Roeh (Seer)-Discernment, dreams. Roeh means "to see" or "to perceive." It is generally used to describe one who is a revealer of secrets, one who envisions.

The information contained within this chapter is not all inclusive regarding the prophet. The brevity of the information provided is for foundational understanding only.

4 EVANGELIST

But watch thou in all things, endure

afflictions, do the work of an evangelist, make full

proof of thy ministry. (2 Timothy 4:5)

The five-fold ascension gift of the Evangelist is an accepted office within many of the main stream denominational evangelical circles. It is a less controversial office when compared to the office of Apostle and Prophet. 2. The word evangelist is found 2 times in the Bible (**Acts 21:8; 2 Timothy**

2:5). The word evangelist comes from the Greek word "euaggelistes", which means a bringer of good tidings. This is a name given to the New Testament heralds of salvation through Christ who are not apostles.

The office of evangelist is different from the mandate given to all believers in the Great Commission, which is the command that all believers have to be bearers and witnesses of the Gospel. While all of us are commanded to share the Gospel, the evangelist moves in a grace to specifically bear and witness of Christ through ministry. The word 'evangelist' means one who brings good news, good tidings, and more specifically, the whole good news through the Gospel. An evangelist is one who has a special grace to carry the message of the good news about Christ to the world, especially to the unbelievers. The office of the evangelist and evangelism are not one in the same. All believers are to practice evangelism, but not all believers are evangelists.

The office of the evangelist is unique to the New Testament leadership structure, in that its purpose is to tell of Christ. We do not read of a specific way in which the evangelist is called to this office within the New Testament (i.e., by a dream or direct call of God); unlike the apostle and prophet. The fruit bore by evangelists are an ability to reach out to the unbeliever and believer, knowing where to go for the harvest of souls (**Acts 8:26-29**), recognize that preaching Christ is the primary duty of an evangelist (**Acts 8:5**); provide concrete proof of Christ's Sonship and Messiahship (**Acts 8:27-35**); proclaim the Gospel successfully (**Acts 8:37**); present maturity and balance in faith (**Ephesians 4:11-16**); present a willingness to work with other ministries, including others within ministerial office (**Acts 8:13-25**); have the ability to teach both crowds and one-on-one (**Acts 8:5-6, Acts 8:27-30**); and have a deep concern for those who do not know the Lord (**Acts 8:5-6**).

Evangelists are not stationary. Although they may be a member of a local assembly, they are commanded to go forth with the Word of God. The pastors are stationary. The purpose and sound of the Gospel message coming from an evangelist is distinct. It differs from that of the apostle, prophet, pastor, and teacher. Unlike apostles and prophets, evangelists are often independent. They are called to be accountable for what they teach in their ministries, because they do not have the direct teaching of the Lord that apostles and prophets have. Evangelists must study with apostles and prophets to be thoroughly equipped for their ministry (**2 Timothy 4:5**).

Evangelists, just as the other ascension gifts, have duties that must be fulfilled. Some of the duties are: teaching and preaching to unbelievers (**Acts 8:5-6**); work itinerantly, traveling from location to location (**Acts 8:40**); awaken all (believer or unbeliever) that are backslidden or lost in sin and convict to repentance, bringing about the fruit of salvation (**Mark 1:1-5**); baptize new members, emphasizing the importance and heart of baptism (**Acts 8:38-39**); teach on water baptism (**Acts 8:12**); teach on the life and work of Christ, both in the Old and New Testaments (**Acts 8:30-37**); work in the area of basic apologetics, having the ability to answer questions about faith and offer pragmatic answers (**Acts 8:34-35**); bring joy to others due to the fruit of repentance (**Acts 8:8**); offer assistance and cooperation with others in ministry (**Acts 8: 13-25**); train the church in matters of evangelism and witnessing (**2 Timothy 4:5**); operate in the gifts of the Spirit, especially healing (**Acts 8:6-8**); and operate ministry for the purposes of charity to the poor and less fortunate (**2 Timothy 4:5**).

> ➢ Teaching and preaching to unbelievers

> ➢ Work itinerantly

> ➢ Awaken all that are backslidden

> ➢ Awaken those that are lost

➢ Bring about the fruit of salvation

➢ Baptize new members

➢ Teach on water baptism

➢ Teach on the life and work of Christ, both in the Old and New Testaments

➢ Work in the area of basic apologetics

➢ Have the ability to answer questions about faith and offer pragmatic answers

➢ Bring joy to others due to the fruit of repentance

➢ Offer assistance and cooperation with others in ministry

➢ Train the church in matters of evangelism and witnessing

➢ Operate in the gifts of the Spirit, especially healing

➢ Operate ministry for the purposes of charity to the poor and less fortunate

We only have one recorded name for an evangelist

in the Bible. Philip is specifically named as an evangelist in **Acts 21:8**. Historical writings and non-canonical works prove that others served in this office (both men and women). The office of evangelist is relevant today, because the call to proclaim the Gospel to every creature requires those that are equipped to perform this duty. It is also necessary that the evangelist continue to train the church in evangelism (**Isaiah 61:1-3**).

5 PASTOR

And I will give you pastors according to mine heart, which shall feed you with knowledge and understanding. And it shall come to pass, when ye be multiplied and increased in the land, in those days, saith the LORD, they shall say no more, The ark of the covenant of the LORD: neither shall it come to mind: neither shall they remember it; neither shall they visit it; neither shall that be done any more. (**Jeremiah 3:15-16**)

One of the least controversial offices within the five-fold

ascension gifts given to the church is the office of the pastor. This office has been accepted across the majority of the denominational lines that have been set. The majority of controversy that arises from this office comes stems from the place of a woman being within this particular office. The church has come a long way in accepting women within leadership positions such as teaching, or more of cleaning, cooking, children's ministry, etc. However, many women are still fought regarding this particular position. Depending upon the denomination, this is the position of the set man or woman.

This chapter begins with the Scripture passage of **Jeremiah 3:15-16**. Jeremiah was a type of pastor. His call, function, and work centered on the lost people of Israel, who functioned without truth and guidance. Israel was lost due to improper leadership. Jeremiah prophesied a time when the people would be rightly led by pastors that were selected and given by God Himself.

Pastors-from the Hebrew word "ra'ah", which means to pasture, tend, graze, feed; to associate with, be a friend of (meaning probable); to be a special friend. The word "pastor" is found only one time in the New Testament in Ephesians 4:11. We do see the word "pastor" present in the Old Testament, especially in the book of Jeremiah (**Jeremiah 3:15-16**). Because the word is only used one time the office is commonly confused with the offices of elder, overseer, or bishop. These offices are not the pastoral office. These different terms represent different purposes, ranks, and work within a church; and represents different leadership roles.

The term refer to different work (bishops, elders, and deacons are all appointment ministries, ministries established to be "helps" to the five-fold), although in many instances, they do overlap. The Scripture suggests elders oversaw the responsibilities of a congregation, a pastor was the "shepherd" of the people, attending to their various spiritual needs, and a bishop may have overseen more than one church or held a senior position as an overseer.

The Bible does not indicate how many pastors a church should have. It can recognized that a church may have pastors function to oversee different church ministries. Examples include youth ministry pastors, women's ministry pastors, men's ministry pastors, and so on. The primary grace of the pastoral office is caring for God's people, meeting their spiritual needs (**Jeremiah 3:15-16**). Pastors are called to have a heart for the people that

they serve, as they meet spiritual needs in love and purpose (**Psalm 23:1-6**). They are not the foundation of a church, as are apostles and prophets. Therefore, you cannot build a church on the foundation of a pastor or many pastors- that is not a part of God's order. Therefore, not being the supreme authority, the pastor learns the truth of the Word through the apostles and prophets.

The comparison of the pastor to a shepherd gives us an idea of how people saw the call, and also helps us to see the way a shepherd cares for and tends the flock they are given as the way pastors are called to lead God's people. There will be people who seek to exploit and mislead the people of God. That's why the people of God who are called to pastor are compared to shepherds. Calling a pastor a 'shepherd' speaks both of his or her call and work, and the people they are called to lead. A shepherd must be patient with sheep; who tend to be stubborn, ignorant, and self-destructive. The shepherd's heart is one of love and concern, care and tending, and feeding and provision. If God provides pastors after His own heart, this means that the pastor's heart is inclined for his or her people; as God's heart is inclined towards us His people. It is the pastor's job to lead with knowledge and understanding, requiring the pastor to have that as well. When we have pastors who lead according to God's heart, the need for law fades, because truth and reality reigns in the hearts of God's people.

A pastor is called to pastor a local church community. This is different from apostles and prophets, who instruct and establish the foundations of the church through leadership (**Ephesians 2:20**) ; and evangelists, who build up the church by reaching those who need to learn more of the Lord, or develop a deeper walk with Him (**Acts 8:26-40**). It is the pastor's job to care for the people, walking after God's own heart. Pastors are called by God for the purpose of providing knowledge and understanding to the people. Pastors are called to be agents of unity, uniting the flock rather than causing it to scatter. Rather than be destroyers of the vineyard, pastors help care for and tend it. Instead of bringing desolation, pastors are called to bring forth life and restoration. Pastors are called to have a powerful heart of compassion and love toward those they lead

(**Jeremiah 12:10-17**). Pastors are not called to be brutish, nor abusive in their leadership(**Jeremiah 10:19-25**).

Pastoring is the only office of the five-fold that mentions the prosperity of the people in a repeated way (**3 John 1:2**). As the Word tells us to prosper, even as our souls prosper, so the pastor is called to be an agent of prosperity, fruitfulness, and increase (**Psalms 23:5-6**). This is because as a shepherd tends the flock, they work so none are lost and the flock increases in number. This means a healthy congregation reflects spiritual health and health in every area of their lives leading to a blessed and prosperous living (**Jeremiah 23:1-4**).

The duties of the pastor include: Love and care for the flock of God (**Jeremiah 3:15-16**); spiritually feed the flock of God through teaching (**Jeremiah 17:13-27**); teach and instruct in the ways of God, that they may be clear (**Acts 18:18-28**); lead in the ways of righteousness and knowledge (**Jeremiah 3:15-16**); work in the ministry of restoration (**Psalm 23:3**); encourage (**Psalm 23:3-6**); handle matters of local church discipline and mediation (**Matthew 18:15-17**); assist the apostles and prophets upon their visit to a local assembly (**Acts 16:14-15**); refute falsehood and false leadership (**Jeremiah 17:13-27; Jeremiah 23:1-4**); and walk in the gifts of the Spirit (**Romans 12:6-8**).

- ➤ Love and care for the flock of God
- ➤ Spiritually feed the flock of God through teaching
- ➤ Teach and instruct in the ways of God, that they may be clear;
- ➤ Lead in ways of righteousness and knowledge
- ➤ Work in the ministry of restoration
- ➤ Encourage
- ➤ Handle matters of local church discipline and mediation
- ➤ Assist the apostles and prophets upon their visit to a local assembly
- ➤ Refute falsehood and false leadership

➢ Walk in the gifts of the Spirit

No individual is named as pastor in the New Testament (except Christ Good Shepherd). While the role of the pastor is not as debated as the office of the apostle and/or prophet, it is misunderstood. The biblical standards for pastors must be followed for the successful continuation of the church **(1 Peter 5:1-10, 1 Timothy 3:17, Titus 1:6-16**).

6 TEACHER

Having then gifts differing according to the grace that is given to us, whether prophecy, let us prophesy according to the proportion of faith; Or ministry, let us wait on our ministering: or he that teacheth, on teaching; (**Romans 12:6-7**)

Like the office of prophet and evangelist which carry gifts that can serve in a different function within the church body in an individual who does not hold prophetic or evangelistic office, one can have a gift of teaching without holding the office of teacher (**Ephesians 4:11, 1 Corinthians 12:27-31**). One example was Paul, who described himself as a teacher (**2 Timothy 1:11**). The role of a teacher carries over from the Old Testament as the office of prophet does (**Exodus 18:19-20**).

Ancient cultures had a great regard for teachers and individuals who proved to be experts in thought or a certain area of study. Both Greek and Roman societies held great debates and schools featuring their greatest thinkers and philosophers. It would have been no shock to the ancients, therefore, that teachers were a part of the five-fold ministry, responsible for teaching and instructing others. We know from history that New Testament teachers were often personal sponsors to new converts, teaching them in essential matters of faith, as well as teaching individuals and groups in the church on all different levels and age groups.

Throughout the Old Testament, we see a clear command for the people of God to be taught of God's teachers in the essential matters of belief and faith (**Isaiah 30:20-21**). Even though all of the offices of the five-fold ministry involve teaching, the specific office of teacher acknowledges the grace of teaching to individuals who teach, but do not serve in church administrative leadership (**1 Corinthians 12:27-31**). Teaching is identified as a gift of God's grace. Throughout the Old and New Testaments, we see the important value in teaching as a way to pass on the faith to new converts and future generations. If one is called to teach, then one must teach as that recognizes the grace of God at work within that individual for that purpose.

The New Testament does not list specific criteria to be a teacher. What we can draw for criteria on the teaching office can be found in different places with the Scriptures: Have been thoroughly taught oneself, including on advanced doctrinal matters (one who has not moved to advanced teaching is not qualified for teaching **Hebrews 5:11-13**, be well skilled within the Word, as well as bring about maturity in faith **Hebrews 5:13-14**, be sound in speech which cannot be condemned or contradicted (**Titus 2:8**), show forth a pattern of good works which align with Scriptural teaching (**Titus 2:7, James 3:15-18**), Not blasphemers of the Word of God (**Titus 2:8**), and bring forth wisdom from words (**James 3:13-14**). Teachers can teach believing adults (**Deuteronomy 4:1-6**), children (**Deuteronomy 4:9-10**), youth (**2 Timothy 2:22**), men (**Titus 2:6**), and women (**Titus 2:4-7**).

In James 3, people are warned against taking the teaching office lightly. Those who teach are in danger of greater condemnation for teaching falsehoods (**James 3:1**). We also see a dialogue on the tongue and the importance of taming the tongue (**James 3:2-12**). It is important that teachers, who use their mouths for teaching of God's glory, do not use their words lightly. James 3 shows the important value for teachers to refrain from blessing and cursing from their words (**James 3:2-12**).

The duties of a teacher include teaching the Word (**Hebrews 5:13-14**), showing forth good works (**Titus 2:7**), show the way in which believers should walk (**Exodus 18:20**), and teaching on conduct and other essential matters of faith (**James 3:13-18**).

> ➤ Teaching the Word
> ➤ Showing forth good works
> ➤ Show the way in which believers should walk
> ➤ Teaching on conduct and other essential matters of faith

Although no one is named as a teacher in the New Testament office of teacher, the office of teacher was held by both men and women as we can see from the Scriptures. Many today lump the offices of pastor and teacher together, believing they form a singular office. The Greek of **Ephesians 4:11** does not recognize this unity, and therefore we do not see teachers honored in their proper context. Teachers comprise an important function in the body, which should be valued rather than dismissed. Paul list the office of teaching as third in importance.

ABOUT THE AUTHOR

Dr. Theresa Buckner, PhD, ThD currently serves in the office of the Apostle with her husband Herbert Buckner. They currently reside within Arizona with their family. Dr. Buckner is a Christian Counselor and Christian Educator that works around the globe serving as an apostolic overseer and mentor to many ministry and churches. She believes that her mandate is to continue to build up the body of Christ according to Ephesians 4:11. More information can be found out about her ministry at the following website: www.divinelyinspiredministry.com

Made in the USA
Las Vegas, NV
01 October 2021